LET THE PUZZLES BEGIN!

First published in 2014 by Franklin Watts

Copyright © Franklin Watts 2014

Franklin Watts
338 Euston Road
London NW1 3BH

Franklin Watts Australia
Level 17/207 Kent Street
Sydney, NSW 2000

Editor: Sarah Peutrill

Designer: Matt Lilly

Cover designer: Cathryn Gilbert

Every attempt has been made to clear copyright. Should there be any inadvertent omission please apply to the publisher for rectification.

HB ISBN: 978 1 4451 2133 8
PB ISBN: 978 1 4451 2135 2
Library ebook ISBN: 978 1 4451 2901 3

Dewey number: 304.2

Printed in China

Franklin Watts is a division of Hachette Children's Books, an Hachette UK company.
www.hachette.co.uk

PUZZLE HEROES

PEOPLE'S PLANET

ANNA NILSEN

ILLUSTRATED BY
DAVE SMITH

W
FRANKLIN WATTS
LONDON • SYDNEY

CONTENTS

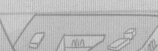

THE QUEST BEGINS

Leah and Zak's dad is a journalist and travel writer. He has been travelling around the world, writing a travel book on the best places to visit. He also sometimes goes undercover to research stories to sell to the newspapers. This time, however, he's uncovered a sensitive story at a gold mine, which has put his life in danger. Can you help to save him?

CHARACTERS

ZAK   LEAH   DAD   MUM

Meet Zak and Leah. They, and their family, are time - and space - travellers. They are also good at solving puzzles!

DAD'S JOURNEY

CANADA

THE GREAT WALL OF CHINA

LONDON   EUROPE

USA

SHANGHAI PORT, CHINA

DUBAI

I'LL BE YOUR GUIDE TO THE PUZZLES YOU ENCOUNTER ON YOUR JOURNEY.

MACHU PICCHU, PERU

START HERE AT RIO DE JANEIRO, BRAZIL

N W E S

LAKE COWAL GOLD MINE, AUSTRALIA

FINDING THE ANTIDOTE!

One day Mum gets a phone call from Dad. Dad has found out that there is a plan to poison him. Luckily he has found out where the antidote is hidden. He quickly sent a trail of secret clues on his mobile phone to Mum in the form of dominoes, which would lead Mum and the children back through all the places Dad has visited in the past 10 weeks and finally to the antidote's hiding place. Hurry and help Zak, Leah and Mum find the antidote to prevent the poison working!

POISON

ANTIDOTE

ARE YOU A PUZZLE HERO?

The mining company sent Zak and Leah another message warning them that if they did not solve all the puzzles, they would not be able to save their father. Can you help Zak and Leah solve all the puzzles and save their dad?

THE PUZZLES

DASH AROUND EUROPE

You'll need these to help with the hotel puzzle on pages 18-19.

 HOTEL PRICE CHART

Lisbon	£40
Riga	£40
Wilna	£43
Valletta	£45
Athens	£47
Bucharest	£50
Budapest	£50
Zagreb	£52
Sarajevo	£54
Tallin	£55
Skopje	£55
Prague	£55
Warsaw	£57
Sofia	£60
Belgrade	£60
Monaco	£60
Rome	£63
Andorra La Vella	£65
Brussels	£65
Amsterdam	£68
Moscow	£69
Bern	£70
Berlin	£70
Dublin	£73
Edinburgh	£75
Vienna	£77
Paris	£80
Stockholm	£82
Oslo	£84
Copenhagen	£85
Helsinki	£90
London	£100
Luxembourg	£100

TRAIN FARE CHART

	£50
	£75
	£100
	£125
	£150
	£175
	£200
	£225

FIENDISH FARMING, USA

You'll need this to help you with the farming puzzle on pages 12-13.

MARKET PRICES

Holstein £8,000   Jersey £5,000   Brown Swiss £6,000   Friesian £4,000

INSTRUCTIONS

1. Count up how much the cows in each field are worth.

2. Compare the amount each farmer spent with the value of the cows in his field. Which farmer has too many cows? Work out which farmer has too few. How can you fix the situation?

MARKET COSTS

Farmer **A** spent £137,000

Farmer **B** spent £120,000

Farmer **C** spent £110,000

Farmer **D** spent £105,000

MILK YIELD PER DAY

Holstein = 25 litres per day

Jersey = 19 litres per day

Brown Swiss = 22 litres per day

Friesian = 21 litres per day

SHANGHAI PORT CONTAINER PUZZLE

You'll need these to help you with the port puzzle on pages 24-25.

FREIGHT CHARGES FROM SHANGHAI FOR 12 METRE CONTAINER

 Port of Hakata, Japan $255

 Port of Sydney, Australia $280

 Port of Hong Kong, China $390

 Port of U.S.A. $3,000

 Port of London, UK $4,600

 Port of Santa Fe, Argentina $4,800

HAZARDOUS MATERIALS INSURANCE FEES

 Irritant fee per container + $650

 Infectious fee per container + $750

 Inflammable fee per container + $1,000

 Explosive fee per container + $1,250

 Toxic fee per container +$1,500

 Radioactive fee per container + $2,000

TEN TALLEST SKYSCRAPERS

You'll need these to help you with the skyscraper puzzle on pages 20-21.

NAME:	PLACE:	COUNTRY:	HEIGHT:	FLOORS:
H Burj Khalifa	Dubai	UAE	828m	163
F Shanghai Tower	Shanghai	China	632m	121
A Makkah Royal Clock Tower Hotel	Mecca	Saudi Arabia	601m	120
C One World Trade Center	New York City	USA	541.3m	104
J Taipei 101	Taipei	Taiwan	509m	101
D Shanghai World Financial Center	Shanghai	China	492m	101
E International Commerce Centre	Hong Kong	China	484m	108
B Petronas Twin Towers	Kuala Lumur	Malaysia	452m	88
I Zifeng Tower	Nanjing	China	450m	89
G Willis Tower (formerly Sears Tower)	Chicago	USA	442m	108

DAD'S PHOTOS:

A B C D E F G H I J

LOCATE THE POISON TRAIL

Dad has laid a rope trail. Each rope has a circle at one end and a square at the other. First, look through the scenes to find the rope that has this symbol at the round end (below). What symbol is at the square end of that rope? Hunt through the book to to find a matching symbol at the round end of a rope following the trail, matching the square end symbol to the next rope's round end, to find the place that holds the tenth and final rope. The poison is somewhere in this scene. Can you find it?

FIND THE ANTIDOTE — DOMINO TRAIL

Follow the domino trail with photos Dad took as he made his journey. The dominoes show a detail of where he is on the left and a detail of where he is going on the right. You find where he went to next by matching the image on the right with a matching image on the left side of another domino. Follow the dominoes to the end of the trail. The last image is a clue to where the antidote is hidden.

The Domino trail starts here.

GANESH

Dad took lots of charms of Ganesh the Hindu god of writers and travel with him but he's left them lying around everywhere. How many can you find in each scene?

THE CHAMELEON HUNT

Zak and Leah bought their pet chameleon with them from an earlier adventure in Egypt. It has escaped again! Can you help Zak and Leah find it on each spread?

MORE TO FIND!

On every spread, you will also be challenged to find charms against the evil eye and Hermes, the Greek god of travel.

BEFORE

AFTER

COPACABANA BEACH, RIO DE JANEIRO, BRAZIL

Dad visited lots of beaches in Brazil to find his favourite for his travel book. Copacabana Beach is four kilometres long and thousands of people flock here every year. It is a balneario resort, which means it offers sports, entertainment, food and much more.

LOST PROPERTY

A large wave swept the beach taking away a number of the bathers' possessions. How many of the following items were lost? Spot the difference before and after to see how many you can find.

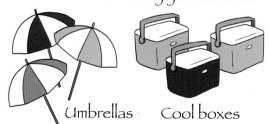

Umbrellas   Cool boxes

SURFERS

How many surf boards can you find before the surfers went out to ride the waves? How many boards were swallowed by the wave?

8

SAND SCULPTURES
How many sand sculptures were washed away by the wave?

FOOTPRINTS IN THE SAND
Follow the footprints in the top picture from the sand dragon to discover which child won the sandcastle competition.

BURIED IN THE SAND
How many people who were buried in sand before the wave hit were uncovered when the wave swept in? Spot the skeleton that was revealed!

Find Hermes the God of Travel.

DOMINO GAME

MACHU PICCHU, PERU

Dad couldn't leave South America without visiting Machu Picchu. This abandoned city, built by the Incas in about 1450, is now a World Heritage site. The Incas built terraces, flat strips of land in steps down the mountainside to grow crops. The buildings have now been restored to give a better idea of what the city originally looked like.

MACHU PICCHU MAZE

You are exploring the ancient site of Machu Picchu and you realise you are lost in the maze of chambers. You are in the room marked with the green flag. See if you can find your way out to the red flag following a red wool route.

LLAMA FLEECE PUZZLES

Llamas live in the hills around Machu Picchu. The local women shear the llamas which each produce, on average, a fleece weighing 2 kg. If it takes 320g to knit a sweater, how many sweaters can be made from the fleeces of this herd of llamas? Count the llamas and multiply by two to get the total weight of wool the herd will produce then divide it by 320g.

SHEARING PUZZLE

It takes five minutes to shear a llama. If one woman in Machu Picchu had to shear all the llamas, how long would it take her?

SPINNING PUZZLE

If it takes 375 minutes to spin a fleece, how long will it take in total for the spinners to spin all the fleeces that have been sheared?

Find Hermes the God of Travel.

DOMINO GAME

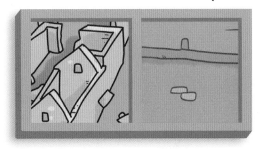

FARMING IN THE USA

Dad visited farms in the USA to write an article on dairy farming. Dairy farming has been part of agriculture for thousands of years. In the past, farmers often kept some cows, alongside other livestock and grew crops as well. In the last 50 years or so larger farms, doing only dairy production, have emerged. There are 65,000 dairy farms in the USA and nine million cows. Cows need a lot of land to graze. The crops grown to feed cows also take up a lot of land.

COW PUZZLE

Four farmers go to market to buy new international breeds of cow. When they get home, they forget to close the gates between the fields. Count the number of each type of cow in each field (see below). Then, using the charts on page 6, work out if any cows have moved and, if so, where they belong.

There are four breeds of cows:

Holstein

Jersey

Friesian

Brown Swiss

MILK YIELD

Having worked out who owns which cows, consult the milk yield chart on page 6 and calculate how much milk each farmer produces per day.

Find Hermes the God of Travel.

DOMINO GAME

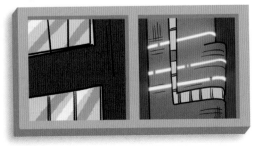

HUNTING WITH THE INUITS, CANADA

Imagine living in the Arctic! Dad visited to find out how Inuit people live with -20°C temperatures and long days in the dark. Inuit people hunt fish with fish spears, standing on ice floes. How many people are out fishing today?

FIRST TO THE WHALE

Hunting, including whaling, is a vital part of Inuit life. Whales provide them with food, clothing and oil. Use a piece of string to find the shortest route for each boat through the ice floes to the whale. Weave the string around the ice floes and measure it with a ruler. Record each measurement to work out which boat will reach the whale first.

PEOPLE AND DOGS

Can you work out how many people have gone on a different whale hunt, far out at sea? Four people live in each home. Count the homes to work out how many people live here. Then count the people to find out how many are missing. Eight dogs are needed to pull each sleigh. Count the sleighs and the dogs to see how many sleighs can be taken out today.

INUiT CLOTHING

Inuit people still wear traditional clothing. In the winter they wear many items of clothing such as mukluks, leggings, gloves, parkas and waterproof boots. They also wear snow goggles with small slits in to keep the glare of the light out.

Leggings

Snow goggles

Parkas

Pairs of gloves

Mukluks

There are 8 types of western clothing to find. What are they?

Find Hermes the God of Travel.

DOMiNO GAME

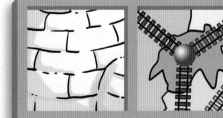

London taxi

Post van

Double-decker bus

Queen's Guard

City gent

Pizza delivery

Umbrella

Telephone box

Dog

FAST AND FURIOUS LONDON

London was established by the Romans in 43CE and is now the most populated area in Britain with over eight million residents. Over 14 million tourists visit London each year. Many of the sites they visit line the banks of the River Thames, which flows through this famous city.

LONDON RUSH HOUR PUZZLE

London is a busy city. Search the city and see if you can find all the things illustrated in the side boxes. Count each one in turn. Remember you have to find them all to save Dad.

FAMOUS BUILDINGS AND LANDMARKS

Which of these famous buildings or landmarks are in London?

HOW MANY OF THE TWO CHARMS AGAINST THE EVIL EYE CAN YOU FIND?

Zebra crossing

Ambulance

Cat

Pram

Postal worker

Traffic lights

Police officer

Ice-cream stall

LONDON MAZE
Can you find your way from the Houses of Parliament to the London Eye? If there are cars, buses or people blocking the route you cannot go through them.

Houses of Parliament

London Eye

STATUES
Which of these statues can you find in London?

Find Hermes the God of Travel.

DOMINO GAME

DASH AROUND EUROPE

Europe is the world's second smallest continent but it is full of towns and cities that are packed with history. Tourists to Europe's countries can see ancient buildings, many different cultures and wildly different landscapes from beaches to mountains.

DAD'S RESEARCH TRIP

Use the photos Dad took for his travel book (below) to plot the route he took round Europe. Make a note of each city he stopped in from Edinburgh to Athens and back again.

Dad stayed one night at each of the cities he stopped at on his around Europe trip. Use the hotel fare chart on page 6 to work out how much he spent on hotels during his trip.

Use the train fare chart on page 6 to find out how much his trip cost him.

Find Hermes the God of Travel.

DOMINO GAME

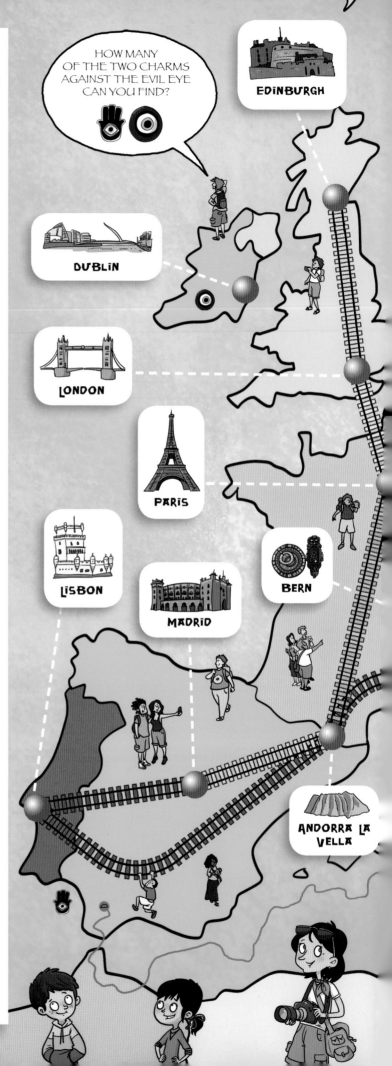

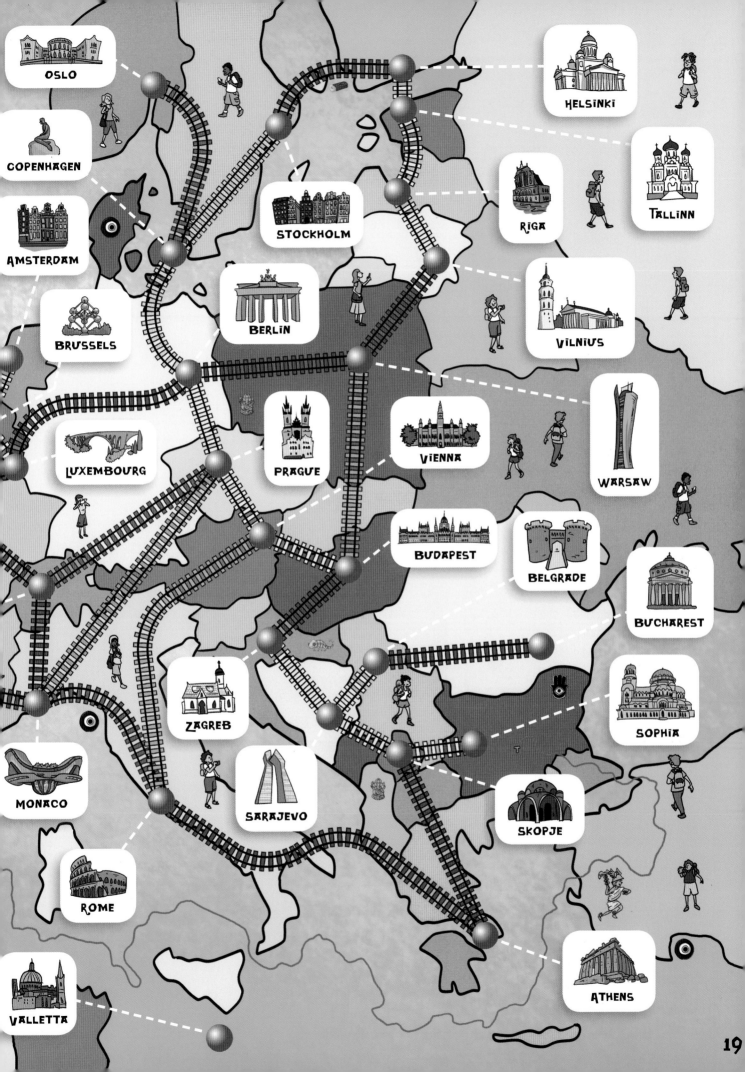

THE TALLEST SKYSCRAPERS IN THE WORLD

Dad visited Dubai to see some of the tallest buildings in the world, including the Burj Khalifa. He took a photo of it at night for his travel guide. He already has a collection of night-time photos of other skyscrapers around the world.

As the population of a city grows, this puts pressure on space so building upwards becomes increasingly important. However, the world's very tallest buildings are often built as a statement – to be the 'best' or to show great wealth.

IDENTIFY THE SKYSCRAPER

Compare Dad's photos of famous skyscrapers with the sections of the photos shown on page 7 to work out which is which. You can also read other facts about these skyscrapers.

 ELECTRIC LIGHT BULBS Count the number of floors that are lit up on each building. Assume that each floor needs 3,000 light bulbs to light it up. Work out the number of bulbs in use in each building.

 Find Hermes the God of Travel.

 **DOMINO GAME**

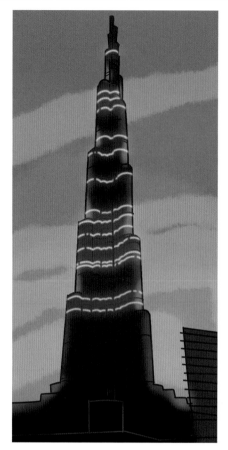

BURJ KHALIFA

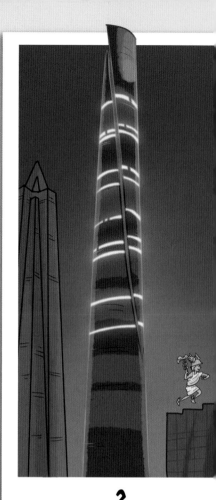

2

6

7

20

21

THE GREAT WALL OF CHINA

The Great Wall of China was built over 2,000 years ago. Since then, many Chinese emperors have added to it or re-built it to protect the Chinese people from their enemies. It is around 7,200 kilometres long. It is made of stone, brick, wood and other materials. Over 10 million people visit the wall every year which has caused some damage to it.

CAUGHT IN THE ACT

Spot the seven photographers in the scene. Work out from the direction they are pointing their cameras which photo below each one took. Which photographer has the evidence to capture a tourist taking bricks home as souvenirs?

Find Hermes the God of Travel.

DOMINO GAME

SHANGHAI PORT, CHINA

While in China, Dad went to visit a port to write an article on the new technologies that help these massive places operate efficiently. Shanghai Port is the busiest in the world and handles over 736 million tonnes of cargo a year. Every month, over 2,000 container ships leave the port.

FREIGHT CHARGES

There are four business executives. Their containers are colour-coded yellow, red, blue and green. Work out how much each business executive paid to export his containers from Shanghai.

Consult the flag chart on page 6 to work out where each container is going to. Consult the charge chart on page 6 to find the cost of exporting one container from Shanghai to the different locations.

HAZARDOUS MATERIALS FEE

Work out which exporter paid the most in hazardous materials fees. See page 6 for the fee chart.

Inflammable   Infectious   Irritant

Toxic   Radioactive   Explosive

Merchandise   Chemicals   Low Hazard

Which one did not export infectious materials?

Find Hermes the God of Travel.

DOMINO GAME

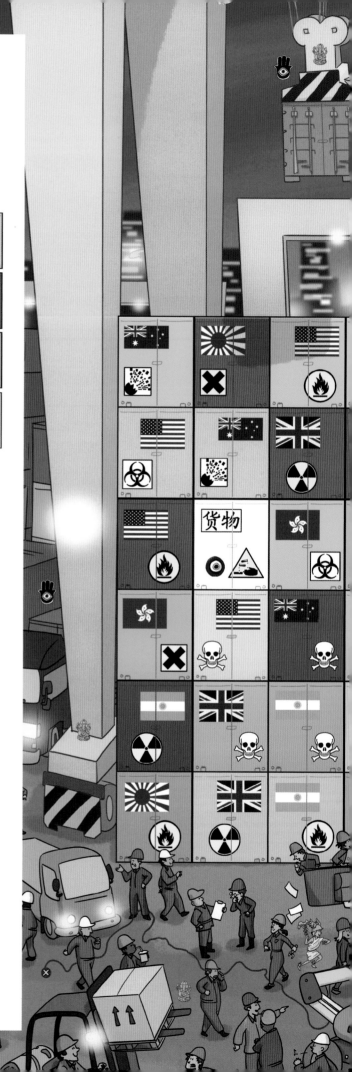

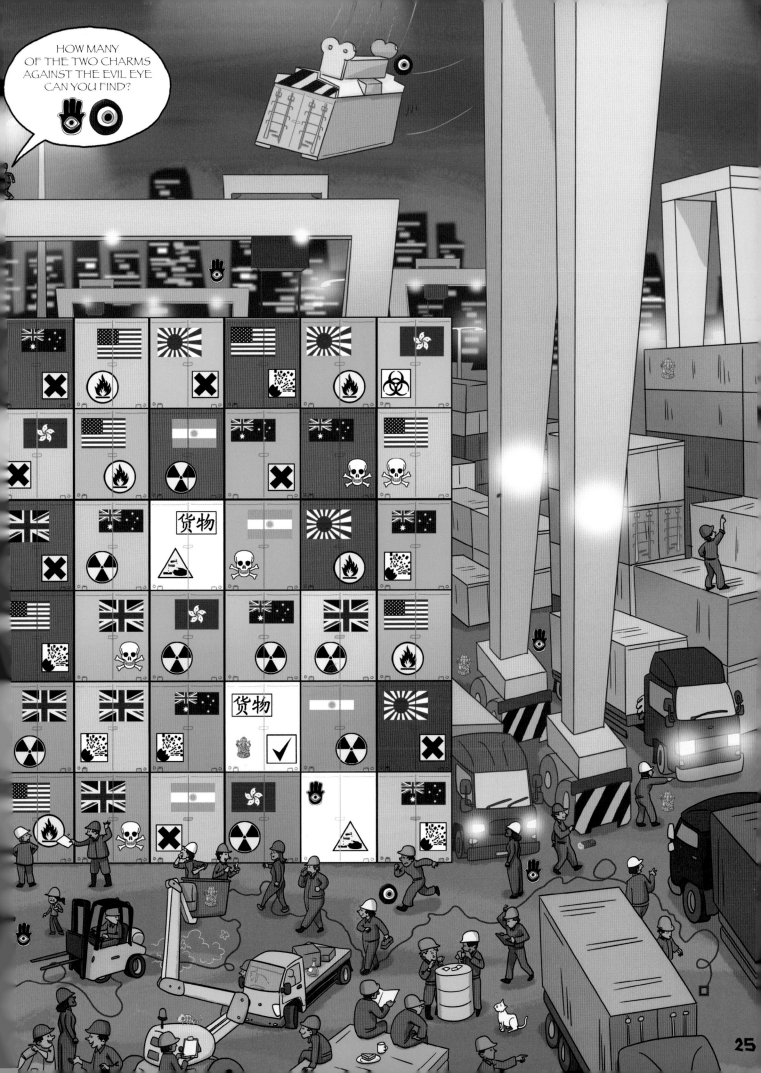

LAKE COWAL GOLD MINE, AUSTRALIA

Dad is interested in the environmental effects of mining, so he visited Lake Cowal, the largest inland lake in New South Wales. The gold mine is a surface mine using open-pit mining methods. In open-pit mining, people and machines remove layers of soil and rock to create a huge pit in the Earth's surface. The mines are dug by cutting benches into the walls of the pit at 4 to 60 metre intervals, giving them a stepped appearance. This helps to prevent rock falls.

GOLD MINE MAZE

Can you find your way through the maze of paths from the green flag to the entrance of the mine with the red flag? You can't go through any blocks including birds, nuggets and vehicles.

BIRD SPOTTING

There are 14 endangered birds at Lake Cowal. How many of each of these can you spot?

Australasian bittern

Black-necked stork

Turquoise parrot

Brolga

Black-breasted buzzard

Blue-billed duck

PETROL PUZZLE

Work out the amount of fuel needed to run the mining machines each day. Count the machines then multiply by the amount of petrol they consume.

Dumper truck
A = 30 litres

Digger
B = 50 litres

Bulldozer
C = 45 litres

Water tanker
D = 35 litres

GOLD NUGGETS

One of the lorries has dropped a trail of gold nuggets. How many can you find?

Find Hermes the God of Travel.

DOMINO GAME
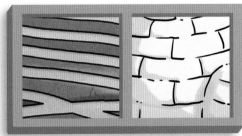

ANSWERS

The pictures show you the best routes for the mazes. If you can't find Hermes, the chameleon and all the charms and statues of Ganesh have another go!

8 — 9 COPACABANA BEACH, RIO DE JANEIRO BRAZIL

LOST PROPERTY
Missing: 5 Umbrellas
3 Cool boxes

SURFERS
6 surf boards are missing

SAND SCULPTURES
4 sand sculptures were washed away

FOOTPRINTS IN THE SAND

BURIED IN THE SAND

EVIL EYE CHARMS x 6   x 4   GANESH x 5

---

10 — 11 MACHU PICCHU, PERU

MACHU PICCHU MAZE

LLAMA FLEECE PUZZLES
There are 16 lamas x 2 (2 kg each fleece) = 32kg.

Each sweater needs 320g so 32,000g divided by 320g = 100 (sweaters)

SHEARING PUZZLE
16 llamas x 5 minutes = 80 minutes, or 1 hour and 20 minutes.

SPINNING PUZZLE
375 hours x 16 fleeces = 6,000 minutes = 100 hours.

EVIL EYE CHARMS

 x 5   x 7

GANESH x 8

---

12 — 13 FARMING IN THE USA

COW PUZZLE

FARMER A	COST/COW	VALUE
Holstein 9	£8,000	£72,000
Jersey 5	£5,000	£25,000
Br. Swiss 2	£6,000	£12,000
Friesian 7	£4,000	£28,000

FARMER A TOTAL: £137,000

FARMER B	COST/COW	VALUE
Holstein 4	£8,000	£32,000
Jersey 6	£5,000	£30,000
Br. Swiss 7	£6,000	£42,000
Friesian 4	£4,000	£16,000

FARMER B TOTAL: £120,000

FARMER C	COST/COW	VALUE
Holstein 4	£8,000	£32,000
Jersey 5	£5,000	£25,000
Br. Swiss 3	£6,000	£18,000
Friesian 10	£4,000	£40,000

FARMER C TOTAL: £115,000

FARMER D	COST/COW	VALUE
Holstein 2	£8,000	£16,000
Jersey 8	£5,000	£40,000
Br. Swiss 6	£6,000	£36,000
Friesian 2	£4,000	£8,000

FARMER D TOTAL: £100,000

Farmer C has cows worth £5,000 more than he spent at market and Farmer D has cows worth £5,000 less than he spent at market. You need to move one Jersey from field C to D.

MILK YIELD
Farmer A yields 511 litres
Farmer B yields 452 litres
Farmer C yields 471 litres
Farmer D yields 376 litres

EVIL EYE CHARMS

 x 6   x 4

GANESH x 3

---

14 — 15 HUNTING WITH THE INUITS, CANADA

FIRST TO THE WHALE
The green canoeist should get to the whale first.

PEOPLE AND DOGS
6 people are missing.

There are 28 dogs so 3 sleighs can be taken out today.

INUIT CLOTHING
You can spot any of these pieces of western clothing: puffa jacket, trousers, trainers, sunglasses, boots, hats, scarf, gloves.

EVIL EYE CHARMS

 x 3   x 2

GANESH x 4

16 — 17 FAST AND FURIOUS LONDON

LONDON RUSH HOUR PUZZLE

 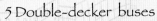

8 London taxis
2 Post vans
5 Double-decker buses
6 Queen's Guards
10 City gents
3 Pizza deliveries
14 Umbrellas
4 Telephone boxes
6 Dogs

7 Zebra crossings
2 Ambulances
9 Cats
3 Prams
2 Postal workers
9 Traffic lights
6 Police officers
1 Ice-cream stall

LONDON MAZE

LONDON STATUES

Eros
Lord Nelson
Fountain at Buckingham Palace
Richard the Lionheart

FAMOUS BUILDINGS AND LANDMARKS

Big Ben   Shakespeare's Globe

EVIL EYE CHARMS
 x6 x2

GANESH
 x5

---

18 — 19 DASH AROUND EUROPE

DAD'S RESEARCH TRIP

 HOTEL BILLS

1. Edinburgh £75
2. London £100
3. Paris £80
4. Andorra £65
5. Rome £63
6. Athens £47
7. Zagreb £52
8. Warsaw £57
9. Luxembourg £100

Total spent = £639

TRAIN FARES

Edinburgh to London £125
London to Paris £50
Paris to Andorra £200
Andorra to Rome £100 + £150
Rome to Athens £225
Athens to Zagreb £100 + £50 + £50
Zagreb to Warsaw £100 + £200
Warsaw to Luxembourg £100 + £100
Luxembourg to Edinburgh £100 + £50 + £125

Total spend £1,825

EVIL EYE CHARMS
 x2 x4

GANESH
 x2

---

20 — 21 THE TALLEST SKYSCRAPERS IN THE WORLD

IDENTIFY THE SKYSCRAPERS

 1. (H) Burj Khalifa
 2. (F) Shanghai Tower
 3. (C) One World Trade Center
 4. (B) Petronas Twin Towers
 5. (J) Taipei 101
 6. (E) International Commerce Centre
 7. (G) Willis Tower
 8. (I) Zifeng Tower
 9. (D) Shanghai World Financial Center
 10. (A) Makkah Royal Clock Tower Hotel

EVIL EYE CHARMS
 x2 x1

GANESH
 x1

ELECTRIC LIGHT BULBS

Burj Khalifa has 15 lit up floors:
$15 \times 3{,}000 = 45{,}000$ bulbs

Shanghai Tower has 10 lit up floors:
$10 \times 3{,}000 = 30{,}000$ bulbs

One World Trade Center has 9 lit up floors: $9 \times 3{,}000 = 27{,}000$ bulbs

Petronas Twin Towers has 16 lit up floors: $16 \times 3{,}000 = 48{,}000$ bulbs

Taipei 101 has 6 lit up floors: $6 \times 3{,}000 = 18{,}000$ bulbs

International Commerce Centre Hong Kong has 10 lit up floors: $10 \times 3{,}000 = 30{,}000$ bulbs

Willis Tower has 5 lit up floors: $5 \times 3{,}000 = 15{,}000$ bulbs

Zifeng Tower has 6 lit up floors: $6 \times 3{,}000 = 18{,}000$ bulbs

Shanghai Financial Center has 10 lit up floors: $10 \times 3{,}000 = 30{,}000$ bulbs

Makkah Royal has 14 lit up floors: $14 \times 3{,}000 = 42{,}000$ bulbs

CAUGHT IN THE ACT

2=E

4=A

6=C

1=D

3=B

5=F

7=G

Photographer **2** has the evidence to catch the tourist stealing the bricks.

EVIL EYE CHARMS

 × 8   ⦾ × 3

GANESH × 6

---

24 — 25 SHANGHAI PORT, CHINA

FREIGHT CHARGES

YELLOW

UK x 3 @ $4,600 each = $13,800
USA x 4 @ $3,000 each = $12,000
Australia x 4 @$280 each = $1,120
Hong Kong, China x 1 @$390 = $390
Argentina x 2 @$4,800 = $9,600

TOTAL: $36,910

BLUE

Japan x 2 @$255 each = $510
Hong Kong, China x 3 @$390 = $1,170
Australia x 4 @$280 each = $1,120
USA x 1 @ $3,000 each = $3,000
UK x 1 @ $4,600 = $4,600
Argentina x 3 @$4,800 = $14,400

TOTAL: $24,800

RED

Japan x 4 @$255 each = $1,020
Australia x 3 @$280 each = $840
Argentina x 2 @$4,800 = $9,600
USA x 3 @ $3,000 each = $9,000
UK x 2 @ $4,600 each = $9,200

TOTAL: $29,660

GREEN

Australia x 2 @$280 each = $560
UK x 3 @$4,600 = $13,800
USA x 4 $3,000 each = $12,000
Hong Kong, China x 2 @$390 = $780
Japan x 1 @$255 each = $255
Argentina x 2 @$4,800 = $9,600

TOTAL: $36,995

- -

HAZARDOUS MATERIALS FEE

YELLOW

irritant x 2 @$650 = $1,300
infectious x 1 @$750 = $750
inflammable x 2 @$1,000 = $2,000
explosive x 3 @$1,250 = $3,750
toxic x 2 @$1,500 = $3,000
radioactive x 4 @$2,000 = $8,000

TOTAL: $18,800

BLUE

irritant x 3 @$650 = $1,950
inflammable x 3 @$1,000 = $3,000
explosive x 2 @$1,250 = $2,500
toxic x 2 @$1,500 = $3,000
radioactive x 4 @$2,000 = $8,000

TOTAL: $18,450

RED

irritant x 4 @$650 = $2,600
infectious x 1 @$750 = $750
inflammable x 2 @$1,000 = $2,000
explosive x 2 @$1,250 = $2,500
toxic x 2 @$1,500 = $3,000
radioactive x 3 @$2,000 = $6,000

TOTAL: $16,850

GREEN

irritant x 1 @$650 = $650
infectious x 2 @$750 = $1,500
inflammable x 4 @$1,000 = $4,000
explosive x 3 @$1,250 = $3,750
toxic x 3 @$1,500 = $4,500
radioactive x 1 @$2,000 = $2,000

TOTAL: $16,400

The yellow business executive paid the most in hazardous materials insurance fees.

The blue business executive did not export infectious materials.

EVIL EYE CHARMS

 × 7   × 3   **GANESH** × 8

GOLD MINE MAZE

BIRD SPOTTING

3 Australasian bittern

6 Black-necked stork

5 Brolga

1 Black-breasted buzzard

4 Turquoise parrot

3 Blue-billed duck

GOLD MINE MAZE GOLD NUGGETS
Trail of nuggets = 13

EVIL EYE CHARMS

 ×1 ×1

GANESH
×4

PETROL PUZZLE

A. 13 dumper trucks x 30 litres = 390 litres

B. 3 diggers x 50 litres = 150 litres

C. 2 bulldozers x 45 litres = 90 litres

D. 2 water tankers x 35 litres = 70 litres

TOTAL: 390 + 150 + 90 + 70 = 700 litres

WHERE IS THE ANTIDOTE?
The last domino is at the Shanghai Port. On the right side, the cross shows where the antidote is hidden.
Can you find it in the picture?

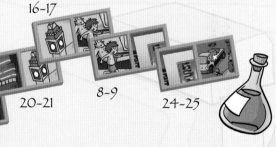

26-27 14-15 18-19 10-11 22-23 12-13 20-21 16-17 8-9 24-25

WHERE IS THE POISON?
If you followed the rope trail correctly it will lead you to Canada.
Look carefully to find the poison in this scene.

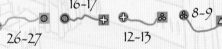
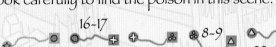

26-27 16-17 12-13 8-9 22-23 18-19 20-21 10-11 24-25 14-15

ONE LAST PUZZLE!

Don't forget to find Dad's memory stick in each scene!

I HOPE YOU HAVE HAD A LOT OF FUN TRYING TO HELP ME. I'M GLAD YOU DID!